. . . LIFELINES . . .

Connecting with Your Wife

...LIFELINES...

CONNECTING
WITH YOUR
WIFE

BARBARA ROSBERG

Tyndale House Publishers, Inc.
WHEATON, ILLINOIS

Visit Tyndale's exciting Web site at www.tyndale.com

Designed by Ron Kaufmann

Published in association with the literary agency of Alive Communications, Inc., 7680 Goddard Street, Suite 200, Colorado Springs, CO 80920

Library of Congress Cataloging-in-Publication Data

Rosberg, Barbara.
   Connecting with your wife / Barbara Rosberg.
      p. cm.
Includes bibliographical references.
   ISBN 0-8423-6020-4
   1. Husbands—Religious life. 2. Wives—Psychology. 3. Marriage—Religious aspects—Christianity. 4. Man-woman relationships—Religious aspects—Christianity. I. Title. II. Series.
BV4528.2 .R67 2003
248.8′425—dc21   2002152201

Printed in the United States of America

07   06   05   04
7   6   5   4   3

The Life Lines series is designed for *real* people in *real life* situations. Written by published authors who are experts in their field, each book covers a different topic and includes:

- information you need, in a quick and easy-to-read format
- practical advice and encouragement from someone who's been there
- "life support"—hands-on tips to give you immediate help for the problems you're facing
- "healthy habits"—long-term strategies that will enrich your life
- inspiring Bible verses
- lists of additional resources—books, Web sites, videos, and seminars to keep you headed on the right path

Life Lines is a joint effort from Marriage Alive International and Smalley Relationship Center. Marriage Alive founders and directors David and Claudia Arp serve as general editors.

Whether you need assistance for an everyday situation, a life transition, or a crisis period, or you're just looking for a friend to come alongside you, Life Lines offers wise, compassionate counsel from someone who can help. This series will connect with you, inspire you, and give you tools that will change your life—for the better!

Titles in the series:
Life Lines: Connecting with Your Husband—Gary Smalley
Life Lines: Connecting with Your Wife—Barbara Rosberg

Life Lines: New Baby Stress—David and Claudia Arp
Life Lines: Survival Tips for Parents of Preschoolers—Becky
          Freeman
Life Lines: Communicating with Your Teen—Greg and Michael
          Smalley
Life Lines: Making Wise Life Choices—John Trent

To Gary,
my beloved life partner and soul mate.
You stand out among all men because
you love and understand me.
I will love, honor, and cherish you
forever.

. . . CONTENTS . . .

. . . ACKNOWLEDGMENTS . . .

Each time I open a book I love to go the acknowledgments to read the list of everyday heroes who supported, encouraged, researched, typed, made phone calls, or showed God's grace to an author throughout the writing project. Any honest person will tell you that writing and compiling documentation for a book is no small effort achieved single-handedly! To accomplish the goal, behind the scenes there is a team of people choosing to give time, talent, and focus to an author. The individuals I wish to thank are my heroes and have touched my heart in many ways. May God richly bless you for your impact in my life!

To Greg Johnson, our agent from Alive Communications. Thank you for inviting me to be part of such a rich and exciting project. Gary and I appreciate you!

David and Claudia Arp, I applaud you for being the brainchild behind the concept of the Life Lines series. Thank you for allowing me to speak on behalf of women. It was an honor. You are esteemed authors and advocates for marriage. We bless you.

Ron Beers and Ken Petersen from Tyndale House Publishers are two men who exemplify the spirit of Jesus in our lives. Your grace, approachability, genuine trust, and dedication to the truth of the gospel, and positioning Gary and me on your radar screen is unmatched. Thank you for always listening and believing in us.

Evelyn Gibson, you are talented beyond belief! Thank you for reading and coaching me to better "speak" man.

George Tracy—no one taught me the bottom line better.

Jessica Parlee, Shelly Beal, Sarah Lemke, Sarah Murray—each of you served me in the most tender of ways. From

．　．　．

typing footnotes, finding a source, or calling an author, no request was too small. I see Jesus in each of you.

Jocelyn Endsley Mulvaney and Sara Sanger—my dynamic duo! You two got into the trench beside me and took on this project as though it were your own. Thank you for your blood, sweat, and tears. Especially to you, Sara, for the night I called you in panic, fearing that with a slip of my hand on the keyboard I had lost the whole document. You not only walked me through the recovering of it but maintained your always gracious spirit.

Doris McFall, my faithful prayer warrior and friend. I can't count the times you called and prayed or even left those spoken blessings on my answering machine. Your prayers upheld me in this project.

Gary, Sarah, Scott, Mason, and Missy, my beloved family. Your trust, rich with love and belief in me, has made me into the woman I am today. I love each of you more than life itself!

And to Sean, who called regularly looking for our daughter Missy. Your beautiful heart tenderly touched my life and reminded me of how greatly the Father loves each of us. In your own way you handed me a cup of water each time you called. I bless you.

And so with a grateful heart I dedicate the following Scripture to each of you:

> "For I was hungry and you gave me something to eat, I was thirsty and you gave me something to drink, I was a stranger and you invited me in, I needed clothes and you clothed me, I was sick and you looked after me." . . . "Lord, when did we see you hungry and feed you, or thirsty and give you something to drink? When did we see you a stranger and invite you in, or needing clothes and

clothe you?" . . . The King will reply, "I tell you the truth, whatever you did for one of the least of these brothers of mine, you did for me." (Matthew 25:35-40, NIV)

Do *you ever wonder . . .*

- why a woman talks so much without getting to the point?
- why your wife's radar goes off when you talk to certain women?
- why you feel as if you're her top home-improvement project?
- why she wants to finish your sentences for you?
- why women insist men stop and ask for directions?
- why women can't just think like men?

When you married your wife, you saw all the wonderful qualities of her femininity. She's nurturing, caring, thoughtful, generous, affectionate, romantic, and gentle. So of course she appeals to you! That softer side of womanhood is naturally appealing. But then you had a run-in with the flip side of her femininity—that sometimes overly emotional, sensitive, moody side that has probably left you feeling confused and maybe even a little miffed. It's that side that makes a man say, "Where did this woman come from?!" Quite frankly, that side of femininity can easily confuse the

· · ·

best of men. There are times when a woman can be just plain difficult to live with—let alone understand!

But the truth of the matter is men and women are different. Now, that's not a news flash; I'm sure you've already figured that one out. But what you may not have known is that God *designed* men and women to be different. In other words, God created your wife to be wired with all those sides of femininity, just like God created you to be the way you are. This is a good thing! It may not feel that way when you scratch your head in bewilderment at something totally crazy—in your view—that your wife's done again. But when you begin to understand the way your wife's been created, and you begin to connect and work with her through your differing designs, you'll discover maybe she's not really crazy, illogical, or irrational after all. And your marriage will be stronger because of it.

DISCOVERING YOUR DIFFERENCES

If you can't understand your wife no matter how hard you try, then this book is for you! It will give you insight into why your wife thinks the way she thinks and appears to act so strangely at times. So let's begin our adventure by looking at a few of the misunderstandings that result from some basic differences between men and women.

. . .

My husband, Gary, handed me this e-mail one day. I think this sums up our differences pretty well. See if you agree.

> Men and Women Are Different: Take bathrooms, for instance. A man has six items in his bathroom: a toothbrush, toothpaste, shaving cream, razor, a bar of Dial soap, and a towel from the Holiday Inn. The average number of items in the typical woman's bathroom is 437. A man would not be able to identify most of these items.
>
> What about the closet? A man has about four pairs of shoes: sneakers, sandals, casual, and dress. If a woman actually counts, she'll find she has thirty-plus pairs of shoes, but she only wears about four of them.
>
> And how about public rest rooms? Men use rest rooms for purely biological reasons. Women use rest rooms as social lounges. Men in a rest room would never speak a word to each other. Women who've never met will leave a rest room giggling together like old friends. And never in the history of the world has a man excused himself from a restaurant table by saying, "Hey, Tom, I was just about to head to the rest room. Do you want to join me?"

· · ·

When a woman says she'll be ready to go out in five more minutes, she's using the same measure of time a man uses when he says that the football game's just got five more minutes left. Neither of them is counting time-outs, commercials, or replays.

Gary and I really laughed when we read this—mostly because it was as if we were reading about ourselves! Gary will be the first to admit he's had to work through the frustrations of trying to figure out who I am—and why I'm so different from him. And I'll be the first to admit I haven't been the easiest to live with at times. I'm sure there were even moments when Gary would pray, "God, what were you thinking? Why did you create her to be so different from me?" But he stuck with me and spent the time trying to understand me. That's made a huge difference in our marriage.

WHY IT'S IMPORTANT TO UNDERSTAND WOMEN

Remember Henry Ford? In the early days of Ford Motor Company, the Detroit plant suddenly lost all its electricity. Ford tried everything he could to fix the problem but nothing worked. Finally he called an electrician. The man walked over to the electrical box, fooled around with a couple of wires, and the power

• • •

was restored. He then handed Ford a bill for ten thousand dollars.

Ford was astonished. "Why should this thirty-second job cost so much?"

"There's no charge for fixing the wiring," said the electrician. "The ten thousand dollars is for knowing which wires to jiggle."

So here's the ten-thousand-dollar question: Do you know your wife's emotional wiring well enough to know what wires to jiggle to connect you with her emotionally? Like you, your wife wants to be understood. She needs to be cared for, listened to, encouraged, and given attention. I feel like a million bucks when I know my husband understands me. When you seek to connect with your wife, you send her a message that says, "I respect who you are and your thoughts, feelings, and ideas." And who doesn't want respect?

HERE TO HELP

So what's the bottom line? Obviously you're reading this book because you want a better marriage and a better relationship with your wife. I'm going to share with you what researchers, experts, and scores of men and women say about a woman's wiring. Keep in mind that because *everybody* is different, I'm going to be talking in generalities or stereotypes, but you'll probably see your wife in a lot of what I'm sharing.

. . .

I'm also going to discuss what I've learned in my own research, through the nationally syndicated daily radio program Gary and I host, *America's Family Coaches—LIVE,* as well as what I've learned in nearly thirty years of marriage to Gary. I'm going to tell you how to tune in to a woman's wiring. I'll help you identify what she needs, how she communicates with other women and with men, what intimacy means to her, and how to understand her definition of romance. I'll also give you Life Support—practical ideas you can implement right away to improve your relationship and let your wife know you genuinely care.

In the Healthy Habits section, I'll present more practical ways to strengthen your relationship and help you understand these six areas that are important to women:

1. The power of intimacy
2. The fundamentals of friendship
3. Safeguarding your relationship
4. Reviving romance
5. Authentic love and acceptance
6. The secrets to really connecting

Finally, I'll direct you to excellent resources to further your pursuit of understanding your wife.

Connecting with Your Wife can be your lifeline to understanding your wife and rediscovering the love

. . .

of your life. So sit down in your recliner, put up your feet, grab a Coke, and get comfortable. But leave that remote alone! You can check the scores after you've read this little book. When you're finished, you'll be saying, "Hmmm, so that's why she acts that way. Now I get it! Maybe she's not really crazy after all."

Is it worth it? Absolutely. My husband, Gary, can attest to that. So whatever you do—don't give up! You'll be glad you didn't. . . . And so will your wife.

... 1 ...

UNDERSTANDING A WOMAN

Men and women sure are different.

When a guy needs encouragement, he typically goes for the slap on the back from the guys on the court. When a woman needs encouragement, she wants hugs from her supportive friends. Men look to their friends to be just company. A woman wants emotional connection in friendships. For her, it hasn't been a good time if she hasn't had a good laugh or a good cry.

Typically, a man wants a friend with whom he can share activities and hobbies. A woman wants someone with whom she can share words. Author and relationship expert Gary Smalley has said that a woman needs to speak twenty-five thousand words in a day—and a man needs to speak only half that number. The problem is that generally a man's words are spent by the time he reaches home at the end of a day, and a woman still has half her words left to say.

Now, I know there are times when you marvel at your wife's talents, abilities, and insights. You wonder, *How does she do it all?* Many women have a tremendous ability to do a wide assortment of things—all at the same time! Like the way your wife can make dinner, grade the kids' homework, give the dog a bath, talk on the phone, and know when there's been way too much silence from the kids—alerting her to a disaster that's about to take place in the basement! On the other hand, there are times when your wife marvels at your ability to focus on one thing at a time. You're probably better able to focus intensely on the project at hand and shut everything else out.

BACK TO BASICS

We can laugh about our many differences, but when you look closely, they boil down to just a few simple principles. Obviously, these are generalities, but on the whole, men replenish by having someone listen to their ideas; women replenish by having someone listen to their heart. Men are more likely to share just the facts, while women love to share their feelings

・　・　・

and all the details—conversations, the setting, what people were wearing. Men compete; women connect.

From the bathroom to the bedroom, it is essential for a man to understand the way his wife thinks. The truth is, God made us different so we could complement each other. If your wife were the same as you, one of you would be unnecessary! So God designed you to pick up the slack where your wife falls short—and he designed your wife to pick up the slack where *you* fall short. He designed you and your wife to combine your unique qualities to become one. (Read Genesis 2:24—"This explains why a man leaves his father and mother and is joined to his wife, and the two are united into one.") But have no fear! God can help you in making that "oneness" a great thing for your marriage. After all, that's what he had in mind when he first created men and women way back in the Garden of Eden. Yes, marriage takes work, but it's one of the most joyful, fulfilling relationships you can have.

> On the whole, men replenish by having someone listen to their ideas; women replenish by having someone listen to their heart.

So let's address some hot topics every man needs to study in order to really understand a woman—and in turn have a great marriage. He needs to understand:

- how a woman is wired differently
- how to listen without fixing
- how women respond sexually
- how a woman's hormones affect her

Ready to tackle these top four topics? Let's go!

WHY IS SHE SO EMOTIONAL?
Understanding How Your Wife Thinks

I've heard many husbands say they can't understand the way their wife thinks. There's a very good reason for this: Her brain is formed differently from yours!

> When psychiatrist [Mark] George scanned the brains of men and women as they recalled a range of emotional experiences, he wasn't expecting to find any major gender differences. "When I did, they were so huge that I hesitated to report them," he recalls. His research showed that the sexes clearly respond differently during emotions, especially sadness. In his experiments, melancholy feelings activated

. . .

neurons in an area eight times larger in women than in men.[1]

On our daily call-in radio program, my husband, Gary, and I reach out to families. We have the privilege of connecting to men and women from across America, many of whom are struggling. Typically, women share their struggles through a myriad of emotions, but when men share an emotion, it's typically anger. When men find themselves at the end of their rope or facing loss, their reactions move from their head—or their thought center—to their heart, their feeling center. A woman also feels anger, but she blends in hurt, insecurity, fear, anxiety, anticipation, apprehension, and a plethora of other feelings. Her reactions are more likely to start in the heart and move to the head over time.

If you're going to understand your wife, you need to recognize that in the realm of emotions, while you think about things and then feel them, your wife primarily feels them first, then thinks through them. That's a vital part of how God created her. So you'll want to accept those emotions, resisting the need to diminish them, change them, or correct them. Bottom line? Allow her to feel her emotions freely. When you do, you may discover that she can help you connect with your emotions as well.

LIFE SUPPORT: RECOGNIZE THAT HER
EMOTIONAL WIRING IS DIFFERENT FROM YOURS

Scientific evidence confirms that men and women are wired differently. Several years ago, for instance, a Canadian research scientist, Sandra Witleson, wanted to detect where emotions were located in the brain. She showed emotionally charged images first to the brain's right hemisphere by way of the left eye and ear, then she showed the same images to the left hemisphere by way of the right eye and ear. From MRI scans, Witleson made an important discovery: A man's emotion is located in two areas in the right hemisphere only. A woman's emotion is located throughout both hemispheres of the brain.[2]

These differences begin even before birth. Recent studies of how the brain works now suggest there are physiological differences between males and females when still in their mothers' womb. Let me give you some background. The brain is divided into two hemispheres and is connected by a communication link called the *corpus callosum*. This fibrous cable communicates information back and forth between both sides of the brain. However, this cable develops differently in male and female fetuses.

At about the sixteenth week of a male's fetal development, the chemical hormone *androgen* washes over his brain. With the microscopic wash of androgen, an amazing transformation occurs: Many of the fibrous connections in the corpus callosum between the two hemispherès of the brain begin to dissolve. Because of this, about 80 percent of males utilize only one side of their brain at a time. A female fetus does not experience this androgen wash, so she is born with the interconnecting fibers intact. That means most females can retrieve and store information simultaneously.

The left side of the brain is more logical, problem solving, mathematical, verbal, factual, analytical, practical, and able to sense fine details. The right side of the brain is more creative, artistic, intuitive, holistic, multiprocessing, and perceptive of emotions. Simply put, the male brain wasn't designed to pass information back and forth between hemispheres like the female brain does. Therefore, it's not surprising that women, with the thicker fibrous connection, can transfer information faster between both hemispheres and can make quicker decisions and judgment calls by utilizing the intuitive side.

> Men's brains are highly compartmentalized and have the ability to separate and store information. At the end of a day full of problems, a man's brain can file them all away.

The female brain does not store information in this way—the problems just keep going around and around in her head.

The only way a woman gets problems out of her mind is by talking about them to acknowledge them. Therefore, when a woman talks at the end of the day, her objective is to discharge the problems, not to find conclusions or solutions.[3]

Wired for expression

The truth is . . . women love words. Not only do they say more words in a day compared to men, but women also tend to be more skilled in their language abilities. In fact, girls typically learn to talk sooner, read earlier, and suffer from fewer reading and learning disabilities than do young boys. Yale professors of

---

SUREFIRE WAYS TO OFFEND YOUR WIFE

Do you know what makes your wife tick and what gets her ticked off? In his popular book, *If Only He Knew,* author and relationship expert Gary Smalley lists ways men offend their wives:

- Showing more attention to other people than to her
- Not listening to or understanding what she feels is important
- Being easily distracted when she's trying to talk to you
- Correcting her in public
- Failing to include her in conversation when you are with other people
- Forgetting special dates such as anniversaries and birthdays

. . .

neurology Drs. Sally Shaywitz and Bennett Shaywitz also attribute this to the fact that a woman can cross-talk between both halves of her brain, while a man generally draws only from his left hemisphere. Because of a woman's holistic use of her brain, she will usually make a fuller recovery than a man will when faced with a stroke or brain injury.[4]

For many women, talking is a way to work through thoughts, feelings, ideas, and problems. It's a wiring issue. Sure, it can short-circuit sometimes. But overall, conversation is a positive way to express and process thoughts and emotions. When a woman hurts, she wants to feel understood and therefore connected to someone who genuinely cares for her. She wants to connect to you.

LIFE SUPPORT: SHOW YOU CARE

Once at a conference I was leading, a woman said to me, "My husband treats his car better than he treats me."

Do you remember your first new car? You were so proud of it—no scratches, lots of zeros on the odometer, that new-car smell, no gummy bears or French fries stuffed in the seat. You washed that car, waxed it, made sure everything looked and ran perfectly. When you appreciate something deeply, you exercise great care over it. The way you attended to that car is how you need to treat your wife.

・ ・ ・

Here are some ways you can show your wife you genuinely care about her:

1. Tell her she holds first place in your life—that she is more important than your mother, your children, your career, and your car!
2. Let her know that you value her opinion, that you want to hear her thoughts and insights, and that you'll act on a decision only after you have considered her advice.
3. Affirm the things she does. When you vocalize your appreciation of her—even in the smallest things—she sees that she is valuable to you.
4. Be open to sharing every part of life with her: home, children, family, friends, and faith. Discuss those topics with her. Listen to her as she shares her thoughts and feelings with you.
5. Hold your wife tenderly—outside of sexual intimacy—just to assure her that you are there for her.

The female brain responds intensely to emotions
Dr. John Gottman, marriage researcher and psychologist, explains, "From early childhood, boys learn to suppress their emotions while girls learn to express and manage the complete range of feelings. . . . A man is more likely to equate being emotional with

weakness and vulnerability because he has been raised to *do* rather than to voice what he feels. Meanwhile, women have spent their early years learning how to verbalize all kinds of emotions."[5]

Gottman also writes, "In order to fully understand why husbands and wives so often miss each other's needs, we have to recognize that the sexes may be physically programmed to react differently to emotional conflict—beginning in childhood."[6]

> A woman's emotions are a gift from God. Be careful not to change them, squelch them, or take them away from her.

Contrast your experiences with those of your wife. She may have been taught that feelings, nurturing, care, and love reflect a healthy relationship. If that is the case, then she can be your greatest teacher in helping you learn how best to express yourself. This is the first step in seeking to honor the emotions she experiences. When she is hurt, an offense has occurred close to her heart. When she is anxious, she senses a threat or perceived threat that appears to be risking her security. When she is frustrated, she may have a need blocked and may not feel heard or cherished. In other words, her emotions are reflecting what's going on in her heart.

Not only are women more likely to express emotions, they are also more likely to respond to emotions in other people. Neuropsychiatrist Raquel Gur

．　．　．

and her husband, psychologist Ruben Gur, did brain scans on volunteers while they looked at photographs of actors portraying different emotions. They found that men simply had a harder time reading emotions. "The subtle expressions went right by [men,] even though their brains were working harder to figure it out," said Ruben Gur.[7]

Understanding this principle is a foundation for the remainder of this book . . . and for understanding women. A woman's emotions are a gift from God. Be careful not to change them, squelch them, or take them away from her. To do that would be similar to her telling you logic isn't a valid way to make a decision. Accept her by validating—or acknowledging as real and purposeful—her emotions so she can safely sort through issues.

. . . 3 . . .

SHE THINKS I DON'T UNDERSTAND
Learning How to Really Listen

Have you ever caught yourself making statements like these?

- "I know how to solve this if you will just listen to me."
- "If your friend bugs you so much, stop calling her."
- "You aren't looking at this logically. Have you thought about how to solve it rather than just how you feel about it?"

Do any of these comments sound familiar? They do to me—because I've heard them in our home! I want

. . .

to help you realize that problem solving isn't a logical process to many women. That's not to say your wife is illogical! It's simply that she needs to think about the problem, feel it, smell it, taste it, and experience it before she can come to any conclusions about it. That's not wrong; it's just different. And that's okay.

LIFE SUPPORT: UNDERSTAND HOW TO LISTEN WITHOUT FIXING

The way we listen

A few years ago, Gary and I were talking after a long day. He was sharing his ideas, and I instantly tuned in—listening, advising, offering suggestions. After all, it works so well with my girlfriends.

Gary turned and looked straight into my eyes. He said, "Honey, I appreciate your helpfulness and enthusiasm, but I'm not your girlfriend. I'm a man. I need you just to listen to my ideas without continually interrupting me."

Okay, sometimes we relate to you like we do the girls—our mistake! But we're not nagging. To the contrary—we're bonding! At least that's what we're trying to do.

You've probably experienced your wife listening—and talking—at the same time. Well, that's what you think she's doing. But actually, your wife is actively listening. She's letting you know she is attuned to you and wants to hear you and help you. She'll nod while you're talking; she'll say "uh-huh"; she'll comment or finish your sentence while you're still talking. From her perspective, she's saying, "Yes, I hear you. I feel what you're feeling. I understand. I'm in your court." But instead of hearing those good things, you're probably thinking, *She's not even letting me finish my sentences! How can she possibly be listening and understanding?* It's important to remember, when the woman in your life begins sharing her ideas and making suggestions, not to take it personally! It's just her way of connecting to you. And you can be assured, she *is* listening.

HOW TO LISTEN TO YOUR WIFE

Want to learn to actively listen to your wife? When you do, she's more likely to grow closer to you, to trust you, to feel as if you're on her side. Here are some easy ways to listen to her when she talks:

- Whatever you're doing, drop it and focus on her—that means put down the newspaper, turn off the television, log off the Internet. (Don't worry, you'll be able to go back to those things!)
- Look her in the eye—that way she knows she has your attention.
- Nod every once in a while to show that you hear what she's saying.
- Verbally connect—just a word or sound ("yeah" or "uh-huh").
- Repeat key things she says to you to make sure you've heard her correctly.
- Keep your body language open—in other words, don't look at your watch or sit with your arms crossed.

. . .

On the other hand, when men listen, they don't usually interrupt or say something until the other person has completely finished talking. And even then, they *still* might not say anything. They may be listening, but they may not express it—either with verbal cues or physical cues such as nodding. To another man that may make complete sense, but to a woman it appears as if the man has checked out mentally and is thinking about something else.

The way we talk

If your wife is talking to you, it means she's crazy about you. It's when she stops talking that there may be trouble brewing. This is why.

Men define their masculinity by separateness; women define their femininity through attachment. Men more often process issues internally. When they do talk to each other, they report. They talk about scores, highlights, events of the weekend, new-car performance—the list is endless. In their "report talk," men condense their stories and edit out the details quickly to get to the point. But because women enjoy the sense of attachment, they engage in "rapport talk." Details are important to women. They don't want the abridged version; they want details, details, details! They want the whole nine yards.

As women talk, they discover who they are and

why they think the way they do. Rather than processing information internally, as men do, women tend to process out loud, through discussion. They resolve issues as they converse. Somehow their hearing, speech, and thoughts are all interrelated, and they need to have all three working at once in order to express themselves fully.

Men are more competitive when communicating stories; women will often downplay themselves in order to strengthen friendships. Women love the details; men love—you guessed it—the bottom line!

Sometimes listening to and processing issues without coming to a firm solution may seem anything but logical to you—like the times when what starts out as a quiet discussion about a family issue becomes tense. Although a husband and a wife may agree logically on what the problem is—not enough family time, for example—they may approach the issue from two different emotional sides.

Take a look at Tom and Margie.

Margie begins: "This family is way too busy with activities. The kids are out the door to football practice, soccer games, and piano lessons every waking hour. We're never home to spend time as a family!"

> **Rather than processing information internally, as men do, women tend to process out loud, through discussion. They resolve issues as they converse.**

. . .

Tom says: "Uh-huh, things have gotten a little out of hand lately. They'll slow down."

"Tom, you're never around either! You've got meetings every night this week. I wish you'd quit saying yes to everything that comes along."

"Margie, we talked about my meetings. You agreed to my being on the school board, and we both knew that would require me to be at all the meetings. You also knew about the kids and their schedules. I don't understand why you're upset when you've known about all this. It will take care of itself; stop worrying about it."

Tom's tendency is to get in there and address the problem instead of acknowledging Margie's emotions—that she is valid in feeling frustrated because she wants to spend time with her family yet is unable to. But feeling misunderstood, Margie gets butterflies in her stomach, her face flushes, and her emotions start to swell. Now frustrated, hurt, and angry, she lashes out, "All you care about is yourself!"

He retaliates in kind. And since the confrontation is going nowhere, Tom turns to leave and Margie collapses in tears.

What went wrong

Here's what Tom could say instead: "Honey, I can tell you're frustrated that we all have so much going on.

What things concern you the most? Let's take a look at the calendar and just walk through some of the plans."

I'll bet that when they finish talking, their calendar looks exactly the same. But by spending a few minutes talking it through with Margie, Tom gives her an incredible sense of relief.

For a woman, connection comes when her point of view is acknowledged, listened to, and understood. When a woman sees her husband willing to open up to her and share with her—and beyond this, to show understanding and a desire to lift her burdens—she will in turn honor him and his needs. Even if you're unable to understand completely why she feels a certain way, it's important for you to acknowledge that her emotions are valid, that she feels a certain way for a reason—and that the reason is real to her. If she doesn't experience that acknowledgment and acceptance, she'll feel disconnected and alone—and no one's needs will be honored. And if left unabated, this relational pattern could leave a woman emotionally unfulfilled—and a marriage dry.

> *Love is patient and kind. Love is not jealous or boastful or proud or rude. Love does not demand its own way. Love is not irritable, and it keeps no record of when it has been wronged. It is never glad about injustice but rejoices whenever the truth wins out. Love never gives up, never loses faith, is always hopeful, and endures through every circumstance.*
>
> 1 CORINTHIANS 13:4-7

• • •

Like Tom and Margie, every couple struggles with emotion and logic from time to time. As women, we want you to help us come to a logical conclusion, but not before you're tuned in to our emotions. I guarantee that if you grasp the secret of what I am about to teach you for connecting to a woman, it will literally transform your relationship!

Let's break this down into three major steps:

- Connecting to her emotions
- Connecting to the facts
- Connecting to the solution

Connecting to her emotions

When you are having a conflict with your wife, you may have the tendency to want to move from the offense to the solution. Quickly.

For instance, Sally tells Dave about a conflict she had with his mom. Dave responds by saying, "Well, if she's criticizing the way you parent our kids, stop calling her every day." Unfortunately, Dave thinks he's helped the situation. Instead, he's added to the stress. Now Sally is upset by her mother-in-law—*and* by Dave, because she doesn't feel as if she's been taken seriously. Sound familiar? Sally would have been more likely to follow Dave's suggestion if he would have listened to her emotions and acknowledged them first. This is the first step in connecting positively with your wife: Instead of giving a solution, begin by connecting to her emotions.

How do you do that? Begin with statements such as: "How did you feel when this happened?" "I bet that hurt when she criticized you." "I am sorry that you are so frustrated with her." "This has got to be hard on you." Even though you may logically be zooming to

---

HE SAID, SHE SAID

Q: Why does my wife change the subject all the time?
A: A man can easily feel confused when his wife changes the course of conversation and traverses from topic to topic in a seemingly disjointed fashion. But to her it makes complete sense! That's because most women have multitasking capability—the ability to converse, listen, and do several other things simultaneously. A man doesn't typically have this ability. His strength comes in being able to focus on one thing and complete it, then move on. While men are more pragmatic and deliberate in their processing, women use the whole brain simultaneously so they are able to assimilate things quickly.

Q: Why does my wife interrupt me when I'm talking?
A: She may interrupt because, from a woman's perspective, that establishes rapport and enhances bonding. She's letting you know that she's committed to you and your relationship and that she's actively listening and interested in what you have to say. Women are more likely to take turns in talking.

Q: My wife likes to talk—all the time. Doesn't she ever need to be silent?
A: Of course women need to be silent at times. But when a woman is crazy about you, she wants to talk to you! That's her way of connecting with you. When she isn't talking, you may be in trouble.

•   •   •

the next level of getting all the facts, if you don't hear your wife's heart first, she will feel misunderstood and frustrated. But when you ask her what she is feeling, she's more likely to feel heard. She'll be able to process her frustration verbally, which will then allow her to move on to the next phase—thinking about the facts.

You can help her process by trying to empathize with her. Instead of coming up with a fast fix, stop and think about how you would feel if you were experiencing what she's going through—just from the emotional end. That's a part of validating her feelings. When you do that, you'll find that she will become more open toward you because she'll feel that you understand her and that you're on her side.

Connecting to the facts

Once you understand what emotions your wife is experiencing, she'll have the ability to look at the facts more clearly. The situation will move from her heart to her head. As she feels heard and comforted by your concern for her emotions, she will be better equipped and able to receive your *thoughts* and *ideas*. Here are some ways you can connect (from Dave and Sally's example):

"It seems like most of your struggles with my mom happen because you feel like you're always having to defend yourself to her. I'm not sure she's ever going to respond the way you'd like her to. How can I encourage you right now?"

When my husband, Gary, and I are in this type of situation, Gary has learned that this is the best time for him to offer suggestions for how he can help. He'll say something such as, "Do you need some space? Would you like me just to hold you or hug you? Can I pray with you? Can we take a walk and talk this through? Do you want me to make some iced tea and we can sit and talk?" When Gary offers a suggestion like one of these, it makes me feel as though he really cares about my predicament. It makes me feel safe.

RESOLVING CONFLICT EFFECTIVELY

Your goal is not to avoid conflict but to work through it. There's no substitute for periodically sitting down and airing issues and feelings with each other and honestly listening to each person's viewpoint. Here are some steps to discuss the issue at hand:

- First cool down. Revisit the issue when you can discuss it calmly.
- Define the problem. Try writing out a summary of the problem.
- Identify who needs a solution and what the other's contribution is to solving the problem.
- Suggest as many solutions as you can. Here it helps to brainstorm. Even write down the silly ones. If you can laugh together, it will help relieve the tension.
- Select a plan of action you both can live with.

When you take the time to work through your conflict, it can lead to better understanding and closer bonds of love.

Adapted from *60 One-Minute Marriage Builders* by David and Claudia Arp

---

Find what part of these tips works for you and begin to help your wife. When you do, these underlying messages will ring out loudly to her: *I am with you. I'm on your side. I love you. I believe in you.* In validating your wife's feelings and helping her work through her emotions, you'll be giving her the ability to look at the facts more clearly.

Connecting to the solution

Finally, after she has experienced the emotions and you both have connected, your wife will feel secure and safe in your relationship and will be more likely to want to sort through some options. Be careful not to try to solve the situation for her. Instead, encourage her to generate some of those ideas. Do this by saying, "What would you like the outcome of this to be? What do you need from me as we sort this out?"

As you try to help her come to a conclusion in her own heart and mind, she'll be more likely to embrace it and move forward. Ask her, "Can I give you some options to respond to?" Getting the okay on the front end helps her to know that you want to help her sort it out, not to fix it yourself. Because when you want to fix it, it sounds to your wife like you want to fix *her*.

I often tell my husband, Gary, that there is a beginning, middle, and end to every problem we face. The

. . .

message your wife needs most to hear is that you're more committed to her than to the issue.

The bottom line is that women are connected to their emotions and are more verbally oriented. We don't need to express hurt or anger and to "talk it out" because we're irrational, illogical, or crazy, but because we use both our minds and hearts to process experiences.

. . . 4 . . .

WHY DOESN'T SHE RESPOND TO ME?

Why the Best Sex Starts with the Heart

Ken had had a hard day. It felt more like he'd had a hard week—all in one day! He drove home exhausted. On his way home from work, he thought, *I'll pull the car into the garage, walk into the house, and loosen my tie. I'll drop my briefcase, unwind a bit, have sex with Debbie, change into sweats, grab the remote, catch some news, and then close my eyes for a few minutes before dinner.*

But all day long Ken's wife, Debbie, had been running to keep up with the kids and a plethora of needs. When Ken walked in the back door, Debbie looked up and their gazes met. His eyes pierced her with "the look."

That "look" in Ken's eye was the proverbial straw that broke the camel's back. It put Debbie over the edge! Ken was no longer the companion and confidant she had looked forward to all day. He was now . . . the enemy! Those twinkles in his eyes sent these messages to her: "Let me have every bit of energy you have left." "Let me take everything you have—and leave you with nothing." "Let me be like everyone else and take, take, take."

Debbie threw her hands in the air and yelled, "No, not now!" Then she stormed out of the kitchen and went into the living room to sit alone for the first time all day.

Does this scenario ring a bell for you?

STRESS RELIEVING OR STRESS PRODUCING?

Obviously Ken didn't mean to make Debbie think he was going to "take all her energy." For him, sex was going to be a release from the stresses of life. But at that point for Debbie, sex was an added stress; it was another thing to add to her already booked "to-do" list. Instead, Debbie needed to connect and talk to release her stress—then she could have sex.

Just like Debbie, your wife probably feels pulled in every direction. Whether she runs a business or the family—or both—she's trying to balance her hectic day while being stretched every which way. She wants

．　．　．

her husband to represent the one person who will allow her to unwind, who will be her friend without expecting something from her.

So how do you do that? Make her feel valued as a *person*. In other words, when you come home, ask her about her day. Ask her how she's doing. Talk to her.

I know some men who groan at this. They say, "I've been talking all day long. I want to be able to go home and *not* have to talk—or listen to someone else talk. It takes too much of my energy." That may be.

GIVE ME YOUR LOVIN'

Your wife needs your closeness, your nonsexual approach that communicates genuine caring. Here are six ways to show her you love her:

- Touch her arm or knee when you talk with her. Your gentle touch communicates, "I'm here. You're not alone. I enjoy you. I'll take care of you."
- Make an effort to spend time alone together—go out to dinner, for a walk, or out for coffee. Show her (and others) that you enjoy the intimacy of being alone with her.
- Grab her hand and hold it when you're out in public.
- Give her a kiss and a hug when you leave and return home.
- Don't see every complaint as an attack. Women think as long as they feel the marriage is working, they can talk about it. On the other hand, most men feel the relationship *isn't* working if they have to talk about it. Allow her to express what's on her mind.
- Recognize her strong emotions as exclamation marks. When she is upset, angry, or frustrated, realize that these emotions are her way of letting you know how much the issue at hand matters to her.

But here's the bottom line: Your wife will respond to you sexually when you allow her to talk to you first. For her, talking needs to precede sex.

As we've mentioned before, if you communicate with your wife and allow her to talk to you about what's going on, about how her day was, about her frustrations, she's going to feel loved, honored, and cherished both verbally and emotionally. And that, gentlemen, is the beginning stage of foreplay. If you try to jump right into having sex without communicating with her first, you may have a sexual response from your wife, but most likely it will be mechanical and compartmentalized. Her body will be there, but her heart and head sure won't. Wouldn't you rather experience *all* of her? Both of you will enjoy sex much more that way.

> When the other areas of a woman's life are in sync, sex is a great expression of a relationship.

If you're still not convinced, consider this: You come home. Your wife obliges you, and you begin to have sex. While you're concentrating on the physical aspect of the act, she's thinking about all the things she has to finish. She has to clean the bathroom, fix dinner and clean up, wash Caleb's soccer uniform for tomorrow's game, run to the grocery store and get ingredients to bake cookies for the church bake sale, make sure Ashley does that homework project she procrastinated on, and pay the bills. Plus her boss criticized her work today, and the neighbor called and complained that your dog keeps running over into their yard. Oh, and she has to make love to her husband—you.

If, instead, you take the time to let her share all those things with you, this is more likely what you'll get: You come home. You ask your wife how she's doing, what she did today, and what else is going on. She opens up to you. You listen. Then later when you make love, while you're concentrating on the physical aspect of the act, she's . . . concentrating on the physical aspect of the act.

In his excellent book *Learning to Live with the Love of Your Life,* Dr. Neil Clark Warren, psychologist and noted marriage expert, says, "The best sexual relationship is one that proceeds out of a couple's deep and intimate 'soul bonding.' Show me a couple for whom feelings and thoughts are shared from the innermost levels, and I'll show you a couple ready to have a triumphant sexual relationship!"[8]

LIFE SUPPORT: UNDERSTANDING HOW WOMEN RESPOND TO SEX

If you want to experience your wife on physical, emotional, and mental levels, then let's begin with this coaching. Until you have received her heart and mind, you will be missing out on all that God created sex between a husband and wife to be. The way women view sex is mental, emotional, spiritual— then physical. Sound complicated? It doesn't have to be. It's just that when the other areas of a woman's life are in sync, sex is a great expression of a relationship.

"A woman is stimulated more by touch and romantic words. She is far more attracted by a man's personality, while a man is stimulated by sight. . . . While a man needs little or no preparation for sex, a woman often needs hours of emotional and mental preparation," writes Gary Smalley in *If Only He Knew*.[9]

Interestingly enough, this tendency can be traced back to the way God created a woman's brain. Some physicians are suggesting that men and women register sexual pleasure in different parts of the brain. Physicians in Scotland have traced sexual response to the right temporal lobe in women and to the hypothalamus in men.

I can't stress this enough: When your wife feels heard, cared for, and safe, she will be more apt to respond sexually to you.

. . . 5 . . .

IS SHE CRAZY OR IS IT HORMONES?

Understanding How Hormones Affect Women

Do you find it hard to deal with your wife when she's cranky and irritable? Because you don't experience menstruation, it's impossible for you to understand fully what women experience with their monthly mood swings and fluctuating energy levels. If your wife is like many women, there are times during her cycle when she cries for no apparent reason, changes her mind erratically, aches, or snaps at everyone for small irritations. All of the physiological factors—the cramping, bloating, and sluggishness—cause her to feel irritable. Some women's personalities change altogether. What's really rough for your wife is that she probably knows she's being erratic and irritable, but she feels helpless to control it. It's not something she can just "snap out of."

Women tend to experience emotional highs and lows because of hormones. For the first twenty-one days after menstruation, estrogen gives women a sense of well-being and a generally positive attitude. And yet, between the twenty-first and twenty-eighth day, those hormones drop dramatically, and with that shift goes that positive mood. Many women become moodier, grouchier, more easily annoyed. By marking those seven days on *your* calendar, men, you could save yourself a lot of tension by figuring out it's not about you! She needs your grace in struggling with her hormones.

LIFE SUPPORT: UNDERSTANDING HER HORMONES

Hormones are a mystery to most men and even to many women. If you lived with your mother or had a sister, you've surely been a witness to the effect hormones have on a woman's emotional and physiological state. PMS, or premenstrual syndrome, is a problem in varying degrees for many women.

When "that time of the month" hits for a woman, stand back and let her express her feelings. Try not to get upset or frustrated when she snaps at you. Ask her about the timing of her menstrual cycle and anticipate it each month. That will help you recognize that her hormones are affecting her emotions.

According to John Gray, author of *Men Are from Mars, Women Are from Venus,* "There is a strong correlation between PMS and the inability to cope with negative feelings in a positive way. . . . One study revealed that a woman's self-esteem generally rises and falls in a cycle between twenty-one and thirty-five days. . . . A woman's self-esteem cycle is not

---

HELPING MEN UNDERSTAND

Q: Since birth control pills are actually composed of estrogen, do women who take them still fluctuate emotionally?

A: It depends on the kind of pill prescribed. In many cases it will be similar to the normal non-pill cycle. Your wife's physician can provide more information as to the particular type of birth control and its emotional reverberations.

Q: When my wife is suffering from premenstrual tension, she not only becomes irritable and short-tempered, but she also seems to become even angrier when I try to tell her everything will be all right and that it isn't as bad as it seems. How do you explain that?

A: By tossing out easy, glib answers to her problems, you're depriving her of the one thing she most needs from you. She doesn't want answers; she wants assurance that one other human being on earth understands what she is going through. She wants to know that you comprehend how tough it is.

Offer her empathy and understanding, helping her express the frustrations bottled up within. Allow her to vent, to cry. Be there for her. She'll feel better knowing you understand.

Adapted from *What Wives Wish Their Husbands Knew about Women* by Dr. James Dobson

---

necessarily in sync with her menstrual cycle, but it does average out at twenty-eight days."[10]

When a woman puts on her business attire, she must be calm despite this emotional tidal wave, but when she returns home, she longs for tenderness and support from the man in her life. A loving man will go out of his way to help her as her hormone levels rise and fall. This is a time when he can assist her by not making demands on her and by offering tender support.

> Women tend to experience emotional highs and lows because of hormones.

What can you do to help?

- Make a special effort to be extra tender. No matter how hard your wife may be to live with, her need for tenderness is ever present. The stakes are even higher in her need for tenderness during her menstrual cycle.
- Be aware that her self-esteem also is connected to her estrogen levels. You may notice she tends to get depressed easily.
- Be prepared for her to magnify problems. Just expect those proverbial molehills to become mountains. But be sure not to contradict or lessen that "mountain." While you may not agree, do what you can to help. This may mean

you'll need to step up your fathering duties to protect her from additional pressures.

- Don't take her moodiness personally. After the inner storm has passed, she'll feel embarrassed about how she overreacted. She really doesn't want to be a bear. She'll need you to give her an extra dose of grace.
- Realize she may cry uncontrollably, sometimes for no reason at all. Allow her to do that, even if she sobs during a McDonald's commercial.
- Understand and be sensitive to her physical discomfort.

J. Ron Eaker, physician and author of *Holy Hormones! Approaching PMS and Menopause God's Way,* writes, "One of the most important steps a man can take in helping his wife who is suffering the emotional trials and tribulations of PMS or menopause is to understand that these changes are real and based on both physical and emotional factors in addition to the stresses of her life situation."[11]

WRAPPING UP

Okay, so you've now discovered that your wife is different from you. God wired you both distinctly so you can complement each other. And what's the best way to develop a satisfying relationship with your wife?

. . .

Listen to her, seek to understand her, and communicate with her. You probably won't always succeed, but keep trying. When your wife sees your commitment to her and your attempts to connect with her, you'll already be on your way to a great marriage.

Here are some reminders to get you started:

- Give her your undivided attention when she talks to you. Put down the newspaper. Turn off the television—don't just mute it or wait until a commercial! Look into her eyes.
- Let the answering machine get the call if the phone rings while the two of you are talking. No one is more important than your wife.
- Find a sport or hobby to do together. This will not only give you physical togetherness but also provide plenty of time to talk and listen. Try biking, walking, or golfing.
- Sit down at the end of each day and talk about all that went on. Refrain from solving problems and just listen.
- Get ready for bed together and go to bed at the same time. You have the opportunity to end the day together, listening to each other and holding each other.

We've made it through some of the basics about women. Now that you know the "nuts and bolts," let's look at some healthy habits you can develop in your relationship. These will allow you to better understand your wife, and in turn, have a lasting, satisfying marriage.

HEALTHY HABIT #1: LEARN WHAT SPELLS "INTIMACY" TO HER

Intimacy is not only important to you but it's also extremely important to your wife. Both you and your wife want it, but you take different routes to get there. In research for a book my husband and I wrote together, *The 5 Love Needs of Men and Women,* the men we interviewed told us they spell intimacy S-E-X, while the women spell it T-A-L-K. How true is that for you and your wife? If you're like most men, you hear the word *intimacy,* and you think of a passionate physical experience. But when your wife hears the word *intimacy,* she thinks about emotional connection and communication.

God wired your brain differently from your wife's;

he wired your sex drives differently as well. Because your sex drive is connected to your eyes, you become aroused visually. But your wife's sex drive is connected to her heart; she's aroused only *after* she feels emotional closeness and harmony.

MEN ARE LIKE WAFFLES, WOMEN ARE LIKE SPAGHETTI

Have you ever considered yourself a waffle? In their book *Men Are like Waffles, Women Are like Spaghetti,* Bill and Pam Farrel explain that men process life in boxes. The Farrels write, "If you look down at a waffle, you see a collection of boxes separated by walls. The boxes are all separate from each other and make convenient holding places. That is typically how a man processes life."[12] His work, recreation, family, wife, church, community activities, food, and friends are all in separate boxes. He can participate in any one of those things without thinking about the other.

> *Be humble and gentle. Be patient with each other, making allowance for each other's faults because of your love.*
>
> EPHESIANS 4:2

On the other hand, women process life more like a plate of pasta. The Farrels say, "If you look at a plate of spaghetti, you notice that there are lots of individual noodles that all touch one another. If you attempted to follow one noodle around the plate, you would intersect a lot of other noodles, and you might even switch to another noodle seamlessly."[13]

To illustrate their point, the Farrels use an example of the workplace. If a woman experiences stress in any of her relationships, she will have a tough time focusing on her job. If a man is having trouble with his relationships, he can tune them out and focus clearly on his work. While personal and professional life are separate things for men, they are interconnected for women. The positive thing about this, though, is that those interconnected "spaghetti strands" allow a woman to multitask—she can manage multiple jobs and situations simultaneously. This is how your wife deals with life every day. And it's probably why you and your wife may not see situations eye to eye.

FROM A WOMAN'S PERSPECTIVE

Several years ago, I invited some women to talk about the importance of emotional intimacy—and a room full of experts showed up! I asked the women how it affects them when their husband recognizes or doesn't recognize their need for emotional intimacy.

One woman offered, "When my husband walks in with that 'look of love' in his eyes—"

"Look of *love* or *lust*?" another woman interjected.

Everyone giggled to release the stress of talking

about this delicate topic. Then the first woman continued, "My initial response is disappointment: *Oh, all he wants is sex.* I feel disappointed because I know my emotional needs won't get met."

Emotional intimacy is so rich, so fulfilling for a woman. It doesn't replace the need for sex, but for her, the emotional need is as intense as the physical need. And when her husband fulfills that need and sustains it through thoughtful talk time, it is much easier for her to move more quickly into a sexual mode.

But what if that doesn't happen? You may not realize it, but when you show disappointment that your wife doesn't respond to you sexually, you send a nonverbal message that she may hear as, "Oh, no. You mean I have to listen to you before I use you?" That may sound crass, but that's how your sexual advances may make your wife feel. A woman has a God-given need to connect emotionally. But if that need is either dismissed or not recognized, she feels that her husband is only using her to gratify his sexual desires—that he doesn't really care about her or respect her as a person.

"I want my husband to treat me as his best customer," said another woman in the group. "He's a top salesman, and he gives his customers the best service you can imagine. When he does that for me, when he shows interest in what I'm saying and looks directly

· · ·

into my eyes as he tracks my conversation, I feel incredible!"

"Yes," chorused the women, nodding and voicing their agreement.

One woman whose husband is a travel agent said, "My husband's mind is sharp. He works with hundreds of people, and he can tell you which of his clients prefer window seats versus those who prefer aisle seats. I wish sometimes he'd remember my preferences that clearly!"

Everyone agreed that after a full day's work, both

QUESTIONS TO CONNECT

In his book *Beneath the Surface*, author Bob Reccord gives a list of questions for you to ask your wife that will help strengthen your marriage:

- Do you know that I truly love you, and do I make that obvious? If not, what can I do to improve?
- Am I treating you as the most important person on earth to me? What could increase that feeling in you?
- I promised to cherish you. Do you feel that way, and what could I do to strengthen that?
- What is your greatest concern about our family, and have you felt free to express it to me? If you've expressed it, have I listened?
- Am I doing anything that would ever lead you to be tempted to compromise in any area? If so, what could I do to change?
- Would you tell me your most significant dreams about the future?

Bob Reccord, *Beneath the Surface*

---

men and women are weary and exhausted. But when a husband reserves all of his attention for work and shows no attention to his wife, she feels weary, exhausted—and unloved. If you don't meet your wife's need for emotional intimacy, you will run the risk of being continually at odds with her. You will get wrath instead of warmth. So be careful about giving your wife leftovers at the end of the day.

Here's what you need to do to experience intimacy with her:

1. Make her feel secure by listening, showing empathy, praying with her, and reassuring her.
2. Engage in thoughtful talk time to fulfill her need for emotional intimacy.
3. Listen to her problems of the day and work through them so she feels safe and secure.
4. Reserve some of your attention each day for your wife. Don't use it all up at work and come home drained and unresponsive. Make her feel as if she's your number one priority.

I know, I know. This takes a lot of hard work. But really, anything worthwhile and good does. Clients don't just show up at your door, begging to work with you. You have to actively pursue them. Your brand-new car doesn't stay clean and well oiled. You have to diligently wash, gas, and tune it. Everything good takes work. If you take good care of your marriage and work at understanding your wife and what makes her feel loved, what helps her enjoy intimacy, then you'll have a good marriage—one that you can be proud of, that you can brag about to your buddies. But, yes, it takes work.

What happens if you don't take seriously how important intimacy is to a woman?

If you don't put the time and energy into understanding your wife's longing for emotional intimacy, the need will persist, and you could, without realizing it, leave her emotionally vulnerable. A woman may end up leaving a man not because of what he can provide but because of what he doesn't provide—an emotional connection. If she feels emotionally unfulfilled, here's what can happen.

> If you don't put the time and energy into understanding your wife's longing for emotional intimacy, . . . you could, without realizing it, leave her emotionally vulnerable.

She will withdraw

Pete's been overworking, then coasting on autopilot at home with his wife, Janie. She feels she's not a priority for him; there hasn't been enough talk time or fun time. They've had a flurry of activities and not enough time to connect. She doesn't know where to

. . .

take all those real issues that need to be addressed, so she stuffs them inside—buries them alive, if you will.

When a woman has continual needs that aren't being met, she will shut down, isolate, and withdraw. When you see an invisible wall going up with your wife, you can bet something is very wrong. From your wife's perspective, it means you are no longer a harbor of safety, but a threat. This pattern of withdrawal can do significant damage to your relationship. And if this remains unaddressed, over time you can end up as two strangers coexisting under the same roof, sharing meals and sleeping in the same bed but walled off from each other emotionally. And the longer the withdrawal continues, the more difficult intimacy is to recover.

Here's a checklist to see if your wife may be withdrawing, isolating herself, or protecting herself from being hurt.

- Is your wife distracted and distant?
- Is she too busy to be intimate with you?
- Do the children or work take higher priority than you?
- Does she have a curt attitude with you?

Perhaps you're missing the mark with your wife by not understanding how to communicate in her love language. When it comes to tuning in to your mate, a great book is *The Five Love Languages* by Dr. Gary Chapman. In this book, Chapman reveals that each person speaks a different language of love. These love languages include quality time, acts of service, words of affirmation, physical touch, and gifts. By identifying what it is that makes your woman tick, you can better convey the respect and love that will resonate in her soul.

WHAT'S A LOVE LANGUAGE?

Here are five love languages. Find out which one is your wife's, then speak to her in her very own language of love!

- **Quality time:** Sharing, listening, and participating in meaningful joint activities communicates that you truly care for and enjoy each other.
- **Acts of service:** If your wife criticizes your failure to do things for her, this may be her primary love language. It could be simple things like taking the car in to have it serviced, replacing a lightbulb in the hall that's been out for a month, fixing the kitchen sink, taking out the garbage without being asked twelve times, or cooking dinner. Acts of service should never be coerced but should be freely given and received, and completed as requested.
- **Words of affirmation:** Compliments, encouraging words, and requests rather than demands affirm your wife's self-worth.
- **Physical touch:** As a gesture of love, this language can be a powerful form of communication—from the smallest touch on the shoulder to the most passionate kiss.
- **Gifts:** Gifts are tangible symbols of love, whether they are items you purchased or made. They demonstrate that you care, and they represent the value of the relationship.

Adapted from *The Five Love Languages* by Dr. Gary Chapman

She will not feel free to respond sexually

A second indicator that your wife doesn't feel understood is that she may not respond to you sexually. Husbands tend to interpret their wife's resistance to their sexual advances as rejection. Often your wife's resistance is not rejection but an indication that she may not feel safe or that she cannot get beyond a conflict the two of you are having. How would you rate yourself at effective conflict resolution?

She may look elsewhere to feel understood

A third consequence of a woman's unmet need for emotional intimacy is that she may fill it with the kids, her career, activities—or she may become involved with another man who will talk to and connect with her. It is the worst-case scenario, but it does happen. If a woman doesn't feel understood and cherished, if her husband isn't meeting her need for emotional intimacy, she becomes vulnerable to other men who do show interest in her thoughts and her emotions.

PUT THE WORDS TO ACTION

Nothing satisfies a woman's emotional need like connecting to her husband. When my husband, Gary, finally picked up on this tip, it revolutionized our marriage. Now when he comes home at night, he takes the time to focus on me. I feel as if he's saved energy for our marriage, and that makes me feel great! And it makes me want to meet his needs. He greets me with a warm kiss and then tells me about his day—conversations with staff, phone calls and decisions, and what he's been thinking about. And he lets me do the same. Some nights we may sound like the six o'clock news reporting about our day to each other: who did what, when it happened. But no matter what, we:

- Engage with each other
- Listen to each other
- Respond to each other's feelings and emotions

Your wife will flourish as she emotionally engages with you. She loves being in the spotlight of your attention. And when she's in the spotlight, she'll see your devotion to her. As she begins to feel treasured by you, she'll also find herself becoming more attracted to you. It's a win-win situation.

. . . 7 . . .

HEALTHY HABIT #2:
BE HER BEST FRIEND

How would you like to take years off the woman in your life and return the sparkle to her eyes? A woman will blossom right before your eyes when you invest in time with her. In his book *Sold Out*, Coach Bill McCartney quotes his pastor: "If you want to know about a man's character, then look into the face of his wife. Whatever he has invested in or withheld from her will be reflected in her countenance."[14]

Few couples today know how to make time to spend together as a couple. Everything is vying for attention: work, kids, sports, even outside friendships. The sad truth is many wonderful opportunities

· · ·

can unintentionally rob you of the closeness you and your wife once shared as a couple.

Family physician Ed Wheat writes in his book *Love Life for Every Married Couple*, "The camaraderie of best friends who are lovers seems twice as exciting and doubly precious."[15] Unfortunately, far too many men and women today are living lonely lives. Friendship simply is not a part of many marriages. Couples dine together in silence, emotionally detached and indifferent. This can happen to all of us—unless we purpose to guard the friendship factor. The same goes for other relationships as well. We can all attest to how easy it is for a friendship to fall through the cracks if we don't invest the necessary time.

To do this successfully, you first need to realize that your idea of friendship may be a little different from your wife's. A woman may not want to go shoot hoops with you; she may not jump at the chance to play a round of golf. A man often seeks *companionship*—a buddy he can hang out with—while a woman will usually seek *connection*.

It may seem as though there's a world of difference between you and her, but a few things remain the

> "Why not make a list of things you'd like to do together to build your friendship? Include everything from an exotic evening out to washing the car together. Put the list somewhere where you can both see it, on the refrigerator or on the bathroom mirror."
>
> DAVE AND CLAUDIA ARP,
> *60 ONE-MINUTE MARRIAGE BUILDERS*

same. Think about the qualities you desire in a good friend. You want someone who's loyal and trustworthy, a companion to enjoy good conversation or activities with, someone who accepts and appreciates you, a friend with whom you can laugh and have fun. Those attributes are important across the board. When it comes to other issues, decisions such as whether to go to the mall or watch the game, that's where you learn to enter her world and she enters yours. So what does a woman really want from you?

ANYBODY HOME? THE IMPORTANCE OF YOUR ACTIVE PRESENCE

My husband works as hard as any man I know. The man's a machine! And when his mind's on work, he's in "the zone." Over the years we have struggled with him being mentally at work even after he's arrived home to the family. One night when our girls were still young, Gary walked through the door following a long day at work and our daughter Missy yelled, "Daddy, Daddy . . . *Daddy!*" But he walked by her and kept going.

"Honey, your daddy's not home yet," I told her.

"But Mommy . . ."

"You and I know your daddy's home. Bro the dog knows your daddy's home, but your daddy doesn't know it yet."

Gary knew bringing his work home with him was

. . .

hurting himself and our family. He realized the importance of actively participating in our lives, and he resolved to solve the problem. Here's how he did it.

Being the family champion

Several years ago Gary was speaking to a group of bankers working with farm families under significant stress during the farm crisis. Gary asked the bankers how they saw their business affecting their families. One of them said, "Gary, I live twenty miles from my bank. I've clocked off the halfway mark between my home and my bank by a telephone pole. I take the first ten miles up to that point to think about my job. But when I arrive at that pole, I switch my thinking to my family. I prepare for our time together. I mentally get ready to greet them and spend time with them. When I leave for work the next morning, I spend my first ten miles reflecting on my family. When I pass my marker, I begin to prepare mentally for the day." Not surprisingly, that man was winning at home and at the bank. Gary says he remembers thinking, *Hey, Rosberg, maybe you need to move twenty miles out of town!*

That man's response made Gary take a closer look at how he was mentally absent from his family when he got home. And that eye-opener caused him to make a deliberate choice to do the same as that man. That choice made a huge difference in our marriage.

So often when a man walks through the door, he's more worried over what's for dinner or where the remote control is than devoting some time and energy to his wife. Why not try that banker's advice? Mark off a place on your drive home when you will make the conscious choice to switch gears and begin to think about walking through your door to your family. If you do that, I can guarantee your family's going to be excited about you coming home!

When you walk through the door, search for changes that may have happened that day. Has the furniture been moved? Are candles lit? Is your house freshly cleaned? Do things look especially nice? Does

---

FRIENDSHIP FITNESS 101

- Cut back on your involvement in some sports activities during the week. Tell the guys your time is reserved.
- Purposely set aside specific times at the beginning of each month to be together. Tell your wife, "We've got a new month. Let's plan our calendar together."
- Cut back on your time working on the computer, talking on the phone, or watching television—and spend it with your wife and the kids.
- Replace an extra meeting that you usually go to and serve your wife by giving that extra time to her. Spend it doing something she loves to do.
- Treat her like a lady. Open the door for her. Help her on with her jacket. Hold the chair for her at dinner.
- Find ways to make each other laugh. Find and share inside jokes and fun secrets to enjoy.

your wife look lovely? Has she done something different with her hair? Compliment her! Even if you come home and the place is a madhouse, toys are all over the place, and your wife looks exhausted, you can still find something worth complimenting. (This is especially important because you have no clue about what happened that day. Remember, she may have been doing double duty—working *and* caring for the kids. That alone should give you reason to compliment her!) Be intentional.

> *Don't be selfish; don't live to make a good impression on others. Be humble, thinking of others as better than yourself. Don't think only about your own affairs, but be interested in others, too, and what they are doing.*
>
> PHILIPPIANS 2:3-4

When your wife has had a hard day—filled with demands at work or the unending needs of your family—when she's pouring out more than what she is taking in, she needs time and refreshment with you. You are her person of choice to refresh her. That's a huge compliment to you! So make an extra effort to *be* home when you get home. . . . The dividends are priceless!

UNDERSTAND HER NEED FOR FRIENDSHIPS WITH WOMEN

Just as you need the guys around to release a little stress or to banter over the most recent game, a woman needs other women around her. In her book

. . .

In the Company of Women, Brenda Hunter writes, "Our friends, especially our best friends, are buffers against stress. They listen to our problems and concerns, and when we leave their presence, we feel better than when we came. . . . Sociologist Pat O'Conner says that women who are rich in friendships enjoy better physical health, live longer, and are less prone to alcoholism, suicide, and mental illness than those who are lonely and isolated."[16]

Few things refresh a woman more than the bonding that occurs with other women. It builds emotional resilience. Here's how you can help her connect with her female friends:

FIVE WAYS TO WOO YOUR WIFE

- Go through the phone book together and each pick six restaurants you've never been to but would like to try. Then once a month, try out one of the places for dinner. One month you pick one of her choices; the next month she can pick one of yours.
- Do tasks around the house together. If your wife is folding laundry, cleaning the kitchen, or doing yard work, step to her side and do it with her.
- Go to bed twenty minutes early, turn off the TV, and hold each other while you talk.
- Run her a bath, light candles, and encourage her to relax while you entertain the kids. Lay her robe and pajamas on the bed—and lie on her side of the bed to warm the sheets for her. Find her favorite magazine and let her relax and fall asleep.
- Say to your wife, "I'm glad you're my best friend."

- Encourage her to get out with the gals and see a movie, go shopping, or grab a cup of coffee— sans the kids.
- Encourage her to invite a friend to a *Women of Faith* conference or a similar event.
- Get rid of the obstacles. You secure the baby-sitting and make sure she gets out.
- Encourage her to gather some girlfriends and watch a video series. There's one I recommend: *The Extraordinary Woman* video series by the American Association of Christian Counselors, www.aacc.net.
- Father the kids. You'll never regret the time you spend with them, and she'll appreciate getting a break from it all.

When your wife is able to hang out with her women friends, she'll feel rejuvenated, and that in turn will strengthen your marriage. Encourage her to enjoy her female friendships.

. . . 8 . . .

HEALTHY HABIT #3:
SAFEGUARD YOUR RELATIONSHIP

Dan and Sherry are going to make it, but there are days they feel as if they are miles apart. That's because Dan hurt Sherry. He didn't intend to hurt her. In fact, Dan thought he was guarding his heart, but along came a female coworker, Stacey. Stacey liked Dan and was drawn to him. Throughout the day she sought out his attention—from asking questions on projects to getting him coffee. It began as business, but she enjoyed his company, and he enjoyed her laughing at his jokes. Soon it moved from friendly chats to more private, personal matters in which Stacey took Dan into her confidence. Then came the "harmless" physical touch, secret phone calls, letters, e-mails, and a handful of lunches. Sex never occurred—but it didn't have to in order to threaten Dan and Sherry's marriage.

When Sherry discovered what was happening, she felt betrayed. While what happened between Dan and Stacey was not a physical affair, it was an emotional affair. And emotional affairs can be just as damaging and painful. Dan and Sherry have been trying to dig their way out ever since.

> **"Every moment of resistance to temptation is a victory."**
>
> FREDRICK WILLIAM FABER

Why is this section in a book on understanding women? As you begin to understand a woman's emotional wiring, you'll recognize the importance of safeguarding your relationship and respecting the boundaries of other relationships. Dan and Sherry are trying to learn to resolve the conflict of broken trust, deception, and lack of boundaries. Dan is honestly trying to learn how to enter into his wife's heart by connecting to her emotions, although he's often understandably guarded. And the sexual relationship that once was super now seems far from reach.

You may never have been through the pain these two are experiencing. Or perhaps you have. Regardless, the same tools you need to develop are the ones these two are trying to achieve in the middle of the storm. These next coaching tips will speak to your heart as well as to your mind. If you have been through the storm, you will remember with some emotion. If you haven't, then you will be on the front end in order to protect your relationship.

KEEPING THE CHEMISTRY WITH YOUR WIFE

Emotional connection is as strong a need for a woman as sexual passion is for a man. Healthy and open sharing heightens the bond of intimacy between a husband and a wife. And that's why you've got to save that degree of disclosure exclusively for your wife.

A word to the wise

Meeting a woman's need for intimacy is vital to a relationship—if it's the appropriate relationship. You may interact regularly with a woman in your work setting, on a community committee, or even at church who is not having her needs met by her husband. Guys, this is not your place to step in and connect to her. Your extra attention, sympathy, or innocent touch

---

DANGEROUS LIAISONS

Be alert. Watch for these danger signals from other women:

- Flattery
- Intense eye contact
- Inappropriate gushing
- Excessive references to your importance
- Talking about intimate topics
- Touching your arm or rubbing your back
- Talking more about you than her husband

. . .

can easily be mistaken for something more when a woman's emotional needs have been ignored.

Women tell me how much it hurts to see their husbands immersed in intimate conversations with other women, giving them the attention these wives crave—and deserve. From appearances it feels intimate—and for some, it actually is. Here's an e-mail I received:

> I walked in to find my husband totally captivated by a woman as she was pouring out her heart about how tough her marriage was. Although she was always flattering him, it had seemed so very subtle. Up until then, my husband thought he had guarded against the "flamboyant dresser," but he wasn't prepared for the subtle degree of temptation that comes from getting comfortable and letting down his guard. They had chemistry, and that opened him up to connecting. My question is, "Is it common for the wife to be the only one to see this?"

Great question.

The female brain is more intuitive

Do women have radar? According to a Stanford University research team led by neuropsychologists

McGuinness and Triban, women do observe sublimi-
nal messages faster and more accurately than men.
Men tend to follow logical analysis of people or
events; women simply "feel" something about a person or a situation . . . and are usually right in those
feelings.

Your wife can probably detect when someone is
upset or bothered or hurt. And if you're like most
men, you probably have no clue about
that unless you see some obvious physical indicator, such as tears or a temper
tantrum. The difference is that women
possess more finely tuned sensory
skills than men do. That's because "as
childbearers and nest defenders, they
needed the ability to sense subtle mood and attitude
changes in others. What is commonly called 'women's
intuition' is mostly a woman's acute ability to notice
small details and changes in the appearance or be-
havior of others."[17]

> *My dear brothers
> and sisters, be
> quick to listen,
> slow to speak, and
> slow to get angry.*
>
> JAMES 1:19

God has gifted your wife with an alertness like radar to protect your marriage. Most women have an
innate sensitivity to nonverbal communication and
the ability to translate it into emotional facts. Trust
your wife's instincts in this area. If she suggests that
another woman is behaving inappropriately, then
there's a very strong chance that that woman is.

Good-guy motives

I trust you're a "good guy with good motives." And you may like to give a hug to a gal once in a while. Unfortunately, you have no idea what condition that woman's heart is in. If a woman isn't having her emotional needs met by her husband, she could easily become set off by the touch of another man—by your warmly touching her. This is also true when dealing with single women. Coupled with affirmation and care, your touch could unintentionally start a forest aflame.

To put it bluntly, it is easy for a man to capture another woman's heart without realizing it. You may think you're just having an enjoyable conversation with a coworker, but she may see it as the only attention she has had all week. Before you know it, your conversations move from friendly chatter to intimate topics. And if she's opening up and sharing her heart, watch out—she is connecting with you. You've heard the saying, "The eyes are the windows of the soul." You can see that open, soul connection in her eyes every time.

Author Randy Alcorn sums it up best in his book, *Sexual Tempation:* "A relationship can be sexual long before it becomes erotic. Just because I'm not touching a woman, or just because I'm not envisioning specific erotic encounters, does not mean I'm not becoming sexually involved with her. The erotic is usually not the beginning but the culmination of sexual attraction."[18] In *Discovering the Mind of a Woman,* Ken Nair vividly writes an account of when he was just being friendly to another woman. It was his wife, Nancy, who tuned him in to the truth: He was flirting with trouble. He listened to his wife's intuition and asked himself some difficult questions to ensure he was safeguarding his relationship with Nancy.

These are some questions—and answers—Ken considered:

Q. What was your motive?

A. I was just trying to be friendly.

Q. How were you being friendly?

A. Well, I was being funny and wanting to be clever.

Q. Why did you feel the need to be clever?

A. Well, what's wrong with wanting to be clever and cool? Everybody wants to be thought of as neat. It's nice to be the center of attention.

Q. Why do you need to be the center of attention with other women?

A. Doesn't every man feel good about women paying attention to him?

This is what Ken discovered: "Yep, Nancy was right— that's flirting!"[19]

You may be unintentionally hurting your wife

Sometimes your actions, though they may be completely unintentional, can cause pain to your wife. For some men, it's the propensity to gaze at other women or to linger too long when surfing the TV channels or to turn your head when a beautiful woman walks past. And for other men, they've slipped a step further into pornography in magazines or on the Internet. Nothing could be more harmful to your relationship.

> *"I made a covenant with my eyes not to look with lust upon a young woman."*
>
> JOB 31:1

Jesus talked about this in the New Testament when he said, "You have heard that the law of Moses says, 'Do not commit adultery.' But I say, anyone who even looks at a woman with lust in his eye has already committed adultery with her in his heart" (Matthew 5:27-28). A woman's inner tendency is to compare herself with whom or what your eyes are on. It causes her to question whether or not she's meeting your needs. She can look into your eyes and see lust or love. A man whose eyes are pure is a man who can meet his wife's eyes with a love that receives her unconditionally and full of grace.

COMMITTING TO HER

Do you know the six words *every* woman longs to hear from her husband? *I only have eyes for you!* Safeguarding your relationship with other women isn't just a maybe—it's a must.

Watch out—it will transform the trust level in your home! You'll visually see her awaken to feeling more beautiful, and you'll reap the benefits of her treating you more lovingly.

How to show and tell your wife, "I only have eyes for you"

When you think of a woman other than your wife, remember what Smokey the Bear says and repeat it to yourself: *Only* you *can prevent forest fires*. Translation: Only *you* can prevent an affair of the heart or the body. Here's how:

1. Listen to your wife's God-given discernment and instincts regarding women who are putting your life and family at risk. Listen also to her strong warnings about how to guard your own heart and what you consciously or unconsciously may be doing to stir another woman's fire. It just may save your family.

2. The next time you're tempted to talk to a woman a little longer, open yourself up, or be stirred by the attention of a charming friend or coworker, *stop*. Think about this section, and *draw a hard line*. I can't be adamant enough. Remember, in the

. . .

Old Testament book of Genesis, what Joseph did when Potiphar's wife pursued him? *He ran*—in the opposite direction!

3. Go to your wife and recommit to her that you only have eyes for her. Those eyes of yours belong to her!

4. Fight the daily battle against temptation with integrity—there isn't a day of your life you aren't at risk. Diligently guard your heart, mind, and thoughts. That's highly honoring to your wife.

By doing these things, you will do wonders for your wife. When Gary reminds me he only has eyes for me, my heart still flutters—even after twenty-six years!

. . . 9 . . .

HEALTHY HABIT #4:
LEARN THE ART OF ROMANCE

Most girls grow up on fairy tales and romantic stories. And while those are just stories, they leave a woman longing for a little romance in her life. Don't get discouraged just yet. It's really not that difficult. Romance is simply a matter of learning what lights up her eyes and puts a smile on her face. Chances are the same thing will work time and time again.

THREE SECRETS TO WINNING A WOMAN'S HEART!
When I mention the idea of reviving romance, this is what I often hear from married couples:

"Romance—yeah, my husband was romantic before we got married."

· · ·

"We had time for romance before the kids came along."

"I'm just not that type—I don't think of those things."

"My mate is too practical for romance."

It seems amid all the distractions of home, work, kids, and life, it's easy to let romance go by the wayside. But romance is a must if you want your relationship to grow into maturity. Without frequent, healthy doses of romance, the relationship will shrivel up.

What's romance? A woman's definition may be something like, "the art of winning someone's (your wife's) heart by lavishing her with your time, attention, gifts, and affirming words." Wait a minute. Sex wasn't mentioned—was it? But if you are an excellent student at romancing your wife and planning

---

ROMANCE TIPS FOR HUSBANDS

- Help her step away from the distractions of the kids, the house, your job, her job, and tune in to her. Schedule time for romance at least once a week. The time will pay incredible dividends in your relationship!
- Listen when she talks about her day, her hopes, her dreams.
- Remind her that you believe in her.
- Cheer her on in her work.
- Declare that you'd marry her all over again.
- Remind her that she isn't getting older—she's getting better!
- Surprise her!
- Laugh with her.

thoughtfully, it will naturally bear out in your physical relationship.

I asked some guys about the biggest challenges they face when it comes to romancing the woman in their life. Some of the responses? Busyness, conflict, distractions, lack of interest, kids, difficulty in coming up with creative ideas, rejection, lack of her affirmation, not knowing how to romance her. Whatever is draining so much energy becomes an obstacle in the relationship.

But here are three winning secrets to romance that, when used, will make you your wife's knight in shining armor. Romance has to be:

> *Place me like a seal over your heart, or like a seal on your arm. For love is as strong as death, and its jealousy is as enduring as the grave. Love flashes like fire, the brightest kind of flame. Many waters cannot quench love; neither can rivers drown it.*
>
> SONG OF SONGS 8:6-7

- Peppered with love
- Seasoned with laughter
- Topped with something thoughtful and kind

The key to romance is this: *Just do it!* Most of these take very little time, and yet the dividends can be great. Here are some starters:

- Go out and buy a Palm Pilot or a Day-Timer and get organized. Every three weeks write down "send

. . .

> **Romance is simply a matter of learning what lights up her eyes and puts a smile on her face.**

flowers"; every third day remind yourself to phone your wife and tell her you love her. Schedule "dinner out," "movie," "picnic"—go ahead and jot it down. Remember, the core ingredients are love, laughter, and romance!

- Try to touch base with her every day. If you can do it at the same time each day, that would be all the better. For instance, at ten o'clock every morning, call her and just say, "Hey, I'm thinking about you. I love you."
- Compliment her—especially for the little things. Go buy her flowers and say, "Thanks for all you do for us!"
- Surprise her with a getaway for the night (or weekend).
- Leave secret notes in her car or at home.
- Fix her favorite meal and include soft music and candles.
- Go for a walk.
- Do an activity with her that she would love. You might not be crazy about it, but do it because you love her!
- Leave her voice mails.
- Give her back rubs—with no strings attached!
- Buy her sexy nightwear *and* flannel pajamas—it'll convince her you do understand her!

- Shower together.
- Take her "to-do list" from her and do it for her!
- Kiss her hand.
- Dance with her in the moonlight.
- Ask her what romantic things she likes—
  and then do them.

What's the winning combination? Genuine love, authentic laughter, and thoughtful, romantic acts are certain to soften her heart.

. . . 10 . . .

HEALTHY HABIT #5: UNDERSTAND HER NEED FOR LOVE AND ACCEPTANCE

Robertson McQuilkin served as president of Columbia Bible College. While McQuilkin held this position, his wife, Murial, was diagnosed with Alzheimer's disease. In his book *A Promise Kept,* he wrote, "As I watched my vivacious companion of the years slip from me . . . our love seeped to deeper, unknown crevices of the heart. . . . But there was even greater liberation. It has to do with God's love. No one ever needed me like Murial, and no one ever responded to my efforts so totally as she. It's the nearest thing I've experienced on a human plane to what my relationship with God was designed to be: God's unfailing love poured out in constant care of helpless me."[20]

Not long after, Robertson resigned as Columbia's president to return home to care for his beloved wife, Murial, on a full-time basis. What an honor, a tribute, and a blessing to see a man step away from what he had worked for all his life to take care of the one who had taken care of him all his life. When learning of this sacrifice, author and speaker Barbara Rainey aptly stated, "Every woman longs to know, will my husband love me with that kind of love?"

HOW TO LOVE HER—NO MATTER WHAT!

Every woman longs to be loved and accepted unconditionally. She longs for someone to look beyond her appearance and even her talents to see who she is on the inside. She wants you to celebrate achievements and forgive mistakes. She needs to know that there is someone to stand by her when times are tough or when life brings disappointments.

> Unconditional love is the commitment that says, "I will stay with you no matter what. I will always love you. I will affirm and support you."

We never outgrow the need for acceptance. When your wife needs your unconditional love, it simply means that she needs you to love her and receive her. Period. For richer or for poorer. In sickness and in health. Unconditional love is the commitment that says, "I will stay with you no matter what. I will always love you. I will affirm and support you." Acceptance means, "I will receive you even in the midst of tough times."

Gary and I have found that our love for each other is glorious in the good times—the vacations, family adventures, and times of deepening intimacy. It is easy to love in good times. But when our love comes under intense testing, we need unconditional love. Love that won't quit. I feel the most secure when I know Gary is there for the long haul. Your wife needs to know that as her husband, you will love her even when she blows it and can't see beyond her pain and failures.

Encourage her

When your wife is disappointed, your first response—your words—will determine whether she folds under the pressure or rises above her circumstances. Your ability to stand with her during times of real trial has the power to dissolve fear in her. Why? Because she knows she doesn't have to face life alone. Here are some phrases that will encourage her:

- "I support you. I'm behind you all the way."
- "I will never leave you or turn my back on you."
- "I don't care what you have done. We can work through it."
- "I love you, and my love will never be something you have to earn."

• • •

- "I forgive you."
- "It's okay. We all make mistakes."

Everyday love

For your wife, it's easy to get caught up in the busyness of everyday life. It's tough to keep up with household tasks, parenting, and working. What are you doing each day to help and say, "I appreciate you"? And men, it's easy to get caught up in working, providing for your family, and doing your own household chores. Sometimes you can forget to say what you're thinking. You assume she knows how you feel about her, but what she really wants is to see it demonstrated.

Here's a "can-do" list:

- Keep a photo of her on your desk and in your wallet.
- Support her in front of the children. Whether you agree or disagree with a decision she's made, take her side in public and talk about it later in private.
- Be accessible to her—always! Let her know how to reach you. Tell her where you will be and when you might be gone. Assure your coworkers that when she calls, you can always be interrupted.
- Remember special dates. Her birthday, your

anniversary, and especially Valentine's Day are extremely important days to her—even if she claims they aren't. Dr. Neil Clark Warren says that on those days, "She wants to feel wonderful about herself. The most successful way to help her feel good about herself is for her to be convinced the man she loves more than any other considers her number one on his most important list. One way a man can convince her that he loves her is to plan before the day, and execute his plan. His actions reflect precisely that she is the most important part of his life."

> *You husbands must give honor to your wives. Treat her with understanding as you live together. She may be weaker than you are, but she is your equal partner in God's gift of new life. If you don't treat her as you should, your prayers will not be heard.*
>
> 1 PETER 3:7

- Mother's Day—you buy the gift. I know she's not your mother, but a gift shows your appreciation for all she does for the family. It also demonstrates honor to your kids.
- Send flowers or chocolates. Enough said!
- Eat together. Don't start eating until she sits down and don't leave the table until she is finished.
- Flirt with her in private and in public. Go up to her in the store if she's wandered off and ask her if she's married. "I've been watching you for a few

. . .

minutes and must say you're the most beautiful
woman I've ever seen." Try to make the clerk
standing nearby blush. Better yet, try to make
your wife blush!

HEALTHY HABIT #6:
MAKE HER A PRIORITY

Tom worked hard all year and planned to treat his family to a trip to Walt Disney World over spring break for a much needed (and often delayed) family vacation. His wife was so excited that she had matching T-shirts made for everyone in the family to wear in the park. The whole family was bouncing off the walls with anticipation. But Tom wasn't prepared for waiting in those long lines at the park. He was accustomed to getting things done—right now! As he stood in line for the rides, his facial expression went from pleasant, to impatient, to just plain mad, to ballistic! He'd had enough, so he left the line and made a series of business calls instead. He planned to return just in time for the ride.

. . .

What was meant to be a fun vacation ended as an expensive family disaster. Rather than coming home refreshed and harmonious, everyone felt hurt and disappointed, especially Tom's wife.

> **A good relationship doesn't just happen. It takes work and more work to make it work.**

So what went wrong? Tom dishonored his family because he saw standing in line as an obstacle to getting something more important accomplished. By allowing himself to be so impatient in line, he automatically became offensive to his wife and ushered toxic poison into the family. They were disrespected. What Tom's family needed the most was for Tom to remain with them in line and tousle their hair, ask them about school and their friends, kiss his wife for no apparent reason, and laugh with the family. They needed connection.

Sometimes a man's greatest strength—his ability to focus and work hard—can be his greatest weakness. Sometimes busyness and good intentions lead to distractions, which soon lead to disconnection. Please remember that when a woman leaves a man, it's not that she is unhappy with what he is financially providing; it's more likely that she's emotionally unfulfilled. As you've read throughout this entire book, a woman longs for authentic connection. Children are the same way. You don't need a reason to connect. Your effort will show them that they are top priority.

Sharon Lavoy of Lavoy's Teamworks taught me this concept: You must be present to win.

YOU MUST BE PRESENT TO WIN

Would you ever consider cheating on your wife or family? You automatically think adultery, and you're quick to say, "No way!" But men, you may, in fact, be cheating on your wife—you just haven't figured it out yet.

In a cartoon Sharon shared with me, a woman is talking to her husband. There's the usual bubble over his head with a liquor bottle labeled "workaholic." What's the bubble over your head? When your wife needs your attention and a listening ear, are you mentally sneaking back to work? logging on to the computer? checking the scores of the game? There are any number of distractions. Listen up: Your family will keep you warm at night—your work will not.

Have you heard the saying, "You must be present to win"? Well, the same concept works at home in your relationships.

It's never too late to make a change. If you have an ounce of air in your lungs, it's not too late. And I've watched my own husband make those needed changes so I could experience safety and trust in our relationship.

. . .

Do you want to experience ultimate connection in your relationship with your wife? Demonstrate an eagerness to be teachable and make some needed changes. Let me assure you—you will never have looked so good and so safe. Tell your wife that she's safe with you! That's right; remind her you're there for her. Let her hear it through your words, and let her see it in your actions. Here's a list of "starters":

- Listen to each other's dreams, ideas, fears, reflections, and hopes.
- Assure her of your confidentiality.
- Validate her feelings and fears.
- Verbalize your love and appreciation in love notes and affection.
- Remind her you will never leave her. Tell her your relationship is the safest place on earth. Love your wife as God loves you—without reserve.
- Make it a priority to spend time together away from the kids. Find activities to do together so you can experience companionship. It's foreplay to the heart and spirit.

A good relationship doesn't just happen. It takes work and more work to make it work. That means you must be teachable and willing to make changes. This takes an investment of your time.

What's your call to action? If you've been distracted

and aloof, make every effort to get back into your family. And if you're reluctant, remember this: No one in business is indispensable. You read every day about the latest company downsizing and announcing layoffs. But there's one place where you *are* indispensable, and that's in your family. Absolutely no one can take your place.

What are you willing to do?

Maybe, like ET, it's time to "phone home." Pick up the phone and tell your wife you're through serving her your emotional leftovers at the end of the day. Tell your family you're sorry that you haven't saved enough energy to give back to them. Let them see that you want to make an effort to change. Yes, at first it may be difficult to say those things; you'll have to swallow your pride. But in the end, it'll be worth it. And while you're worried about your pride, your wife and kids will think you're a hero. You'll gain their respect because you were honest with them. Take a break from all the distractions and spend quality *and* quantity time with your family. It's within your power to change their lives, as well as yours. Isn't it time you got started?

Life is short! Are you giving more to work than to your relationships? Could your wife benefit from more time?

I will never forget the story that hit the front page

of the newspaper when Democratic senator Paul Tsongas from Massachusetts made a decision to withdraw his candidacy in the presidential race in the mid-eighties. I was instantly impressed by the story. Senator Tsongas had recently been diagnosed with cancer, and the reporters asked why he was pulling out of his campaign for president. His simple reply: "No man ever said on his deathbed, 'I wish I had spent more time at the office.'"

Who will surround you in those final dying hours of your life? How would your family describe you: present or absent? I can't say it too strongly—you have to remain present to win!

Go home

Remember those great Motel 6 commercials? At the end, Tom Bodett would always say, "And we'll leave the light on for ya!" Well, for some of you, the light is barely a flicker because it's been so long since you were there. Let me coach you—go home. Go home to the love of your life and rediscover what brings lasting joy, pleasure, and deepened love. Go home to that special woman in your life. Honor her, thank her, and serve her. You may not always have her in your life. Life is truly more precious than we realize.

Briefly, here's a reminder of what you've learned in *Life Lines: Connecting with Your Wife*.

. . .

Men and women have been different from the beginning. Sure, it may seem as if your wife has superhuman powers—seeing with eyes in the back of her head or having an almost psychic ability to know when a wrestling match is about to take place between your children—but truthfully, it's not that she's weird. It boils down to the way she's wired. It all begins in the brain.

Let's not forget hormones. A woman's hormonal fluctuations can have a dramatic effect on her moods, her emotions, and her response to you.

Every box in a woman's life is threaded together. A woman sees every box linked to every other box with an invisible thread that connects them all together. A woman's emotions are connected to her thoughts, her heart, her mind, and her body. When one box is affected, there is a chain reaction that ultimately affects her spirit.

She must connect. Even if you don't understand her wiring for close communication and talk time, her need for them won't go away. She will either shut down or have her need met through another relationship.

She loves a good listener. Your wife's not looking for "Mr. Fix-it" when she opens up to you, because it feels like you're trying to fix her instead of the problem. She's looking to you to listen. True listening

. . .

connects first to the heart, then to the facts. Only then is it time to partner in a solution.

She needs women friends. Her gal pals help her to flourish and provide for transparency and growth. They will rejuvenate her.

A woman craves romance. The romance that started on those early dates needs to continue well into your happy golden years.

In his book *How to Really Love Your Wife,* H. Norman Wright writes, "One of the greatest gifts you can give to your wife is the right to fail and to be imperfect. After all, it's what you want from her, isn't it?"[21] **So lavish her with love!**

OUR TOP LOVE NEEDS

If you've read this far, you may want to consider reading this special bonus section excerpted from a book Gary and I wrote called *The 5 Love Needs of Men and Women*. I think you'll find it an excellent supplement to what you've read so far. We wrote *The 5 Love Needs of Men and Women* to help people understand what qualities men and women need in their relationships. Hopefully you'll find some additional insight into understanding women as you read on.

Human nature is strange. Something in us assumes that if we treat our spouse the way we would like him or her to treat us, we are meeting our partner's needs. But when it comes to needs, the Golden Rule does not always apply. Why? Because in many cases a husband's needs are different from a wife's

. . .

needs. That is most evident in areas like sexual needs, but it is true in other areas as well.

If I asked you if you are meeting your spouse's love needs, you would probably answer yes. In reality, what many of us are really doing is just assuming that our spouse wants what we want, and so we act on that. Often we really don't *know* what our spouse's needs are. And if we don't know what the needs are, we can't possibly meet them effectively.

To help us understand the unique love needs of husbands and wives, Gary and I surveyed more than seven hundred couples. We presented them with a list of twenty needs and asked them to rank, in order of importance, what they needed from their spouse and what they thought their spouse needed from them. Here's what we discovered wives need:

WIVES' TOP FIVE LOVE NEEDS

1. Unconditional Love and Acceptance
2. Emotional Intimacy and Communication
3. Spiritual Intimacy
4. Encouragement and Affirmation
5. Companionship

What your wife wants

Your wife needs your unconditional love and acceptance. Listen with care when your wife expresses a hope or a dream. Ask her to tell you more about that hope, to expound on it. Ask how you can help fulfill that dream.

She needs connection with you. Make an effort to spend time alone together. Go for a walk or on a picnic. Go canoeing. Show her (and others) that you enjoy the intimacy of being alone with her.

She needs spiritual intimacy. Do you pray daily for your wife and then tell her that you have specifically prayed for her? Or even try praying with her. Shared prayer is one of the most intimate things you can do with your spouse.

She needs your encouragement. Brag about her to your friends, to your parents, to her parents, to anybody. Let her catch you at it! She may act as if she's embarrassed, but deep down it will convince her that you really mean it. And in turn it will help build her self-confidence.

She needs your friendship. Spend lots of time playing. After all, if she's going to live with you the rest of her life, why not make it *fun?*

Meeting your spouse's love needs is one of the most important responsibilities you have. Neglecting to meet your wife's love needs could cost you your marriage. Pollster George Barna tells us that Christian marriages are now ending in divorce at an even higher rate than non-Christian marriages (27 percent

. . .

vs. 23 percent). These statistics indicate that just showing up in church isn't going to build a healthy, biblical marriage. You need to know your wife's heart and needs, then sacrificially step away from your own selfishness and learn—really learn—how to meet those needs.

Where do you start?

Take a step towards meeting your wife's love needs. Where do you start?

Take time in the next day or two to ask your wife what her love needs are. One of the ways to begin the discussion is to make a list of what you think her top five are.

Sit down with your wife and say, "I want to learn what your love needs are so that I can meet them more fully. I've made a list and I want to discuss them with you. But what is more important to me is what you think are the most important love needs I need to meet for you."

I recommend picking up *The 5 Love Needs of Men and Women* to deepen your understanding of how to meet the needs in your wife's life more fully.

MEN'S TOP FIVE LOVE NEEDS

Men told us what their top love needs were, too! They are:

. . .

1. Unconditional Love and Acceptance
2. Sexual Intimacy
3. Companionship
4. Encouragement and Affirmation
5. Spiritual Intimacy

Remember that it takes time and perseverance to develop healthy habits. I recommend these resources to help you in your process.

BOOKS

For Husbands

How to Really Love Your Wife by H. Norman Wright

If Only He Knew by Gary Smalley

The Mind of a Woman by Ken Nair

Why Men Don't Listen and Women Can't Read Maps by Barbara and Allan Pease

For Winning the Battle of Temptation

An Affair of the Mind by Laurie Hall

Every Man's Battle by F. Stoeker and S. Arterburn

Guard Your Heart by Gary Rosberg

Personal Holiness in Times of Temptation by B. Wilkinson

Temptations Men Face by Tom L. Eisenman

On Romance

10 Great Dates to Revitalize Your Marriage by David and Claudia Arp

40 Unforgettable Dates with Your Mate by Gary and Barbara Rosberg

199 Ideas and Suggestions to Honor and Love Your Wife by R. Vickers, R. Casey, and J. Sharland

. . .

Dating Your Mate by R. Bundschuh and D. Gilbert

Holding on to Romance by H. Norman Wright

Love, Laughter, and Romance by M. and B. Jonas

More Than Married: 10 Keys to Lasting Intimacy by D. and T. Ferguson

More Book Picks

Do-It-Yourself Relationship Mender by Gary Rosberg

The 5 Love Needs of Men and Women by Gary and Barbara Rosberg

Divorce-Proof Your Marriage by Gary and Barbara Rosberg

The Five Love Languages by Gary Chapman

Holy Hormones! Approaching PMS and Menopause God's Way by J. Ron Eaker

In the Company of Women by Brenda Hunter

Intended for Pleasure by Ed and Gail Wheat

Learning to Live with the Love of Your Life by Neil C. Warren

Love Life for Every Married Couple by Ed Wheat and G. Perkins

Men Are from Mars, Women Are from Venus by John Gray

Men Are like Waffles, Women Are like Spaghetti by Bill and Pam Farrel

A Promise Kept by Robertson McQuilken

Sold Out by Bill McCartney

Taming the Family Zoo by Jim and Suzette Brawner

When Bad Things Happen to Good Marriages by Les and Leslie Parrott

. . .

RADIO PROGRAMMING

America's Family Coaches—LIVE!—Dr. Gary and Barbara Rosberg; www.afclive.com

FamilyLife Today—Dennis Rainey and Bob Lepine; www.familylife.com

Focus on the Family—Dr. James Dobson; www.family.org

New Life Live!—Dr. Paul Meier, Dr. Henry Cloud, Stephen Arterburn, Dr. John Townsend, Mike Marino, Jill Hubbard, Ph.D.

CONFERENCES AND SEMINARS

FamilyLife Marriage Conferences; www.familylife.com

"I Still Do" Arena Events; www.familylife.com

VIDEOS

Extraordinary Women Video Series; www.aacc.net

WEB SITES

America's Family Coaches; www.afclive.com

Barna Online http:/216.87.719.136/cgi-bin/home.asp; www.barna.org

Family Research Council; www.frc.org

Focus on the Family; www.family.org

Heritage Foundation; www.heritage.org

Journal of Marriage and Family; http:/ nefr.allenpress.com

National Marriage Project; http:/marriage.Rutgers.edu

Smart Marriages; www.smartmarriages.com

. . . ENDNOTES . . .

1 Dianne Hales, "The Female Brain," *Ladies' Home Journal,* May 1998, 173.

2 S. F. Witleson, "The Brain Connection: The Corpus Callosum Is Larger in Left Handers," *Science* 229 (1985): 665–668.

3 Barbara and Allan Pease, *Why Men Don't Listen and Women Can't Read Maps* (New York: Welcome Rain Publishers, 2000), 76.

4 Hales, "The Female Brain," 176.

5 John Gottman, *Why Marriages Succeed or Fail* (New York: Simon and Schuster, 1994), 143.

6 Ibid., 144.

7 Hales, "The Female Brain," 173.

8 Neil Clark Warren, *Learning to Live with the Love of Your Life* (Wheaton, Ill.: Tyndale House Publishers, 1995), 131.

9 Gary Smalley with Steve Scott, *If Only He Knew* (Grand Rapids, Mich.: Zondervan Publishing House, 1988), 16.

10 John Gray, *Men Are from Mars, Women Are from Venus* (New York: HarperCollins Publishers, 1992), 120–121.

11 J. Ron Eaker, "What Is She Thinking?" *New Man,* January/February 2001, 54.

12 Bill and Pam Farrel, *Men Are like Waffles, Women Are like Spaghetti* (Eugene, Ore.: Harvest House Publishers, 2001), 11.

13 Ibid., 13.

14 Bill McCartney, *Sold Out* (Nashville: Word Publishing, 1997), 250.

15 Ed Wheat, *Love Life for Every Married Couple* (Grand Rapids, Mich.: Zondervan Publishing House, 1980), 60.

16 Brenda Hunter, *In the Company of Women* (Sisters, Ore.: Multnomah Books, 1994), 114.

17 Pease and Pease, *Why Men Don't Listen and Women Can't Read Maps,* 19.

18 Randy Alcorn, *Sexual Temptation: How Christian Workers Can Win the Battle* (Downers Grove, Ill.: InterVarsity Press, 1989), 17.

. . .

19 Ken Nair with Leslie H. Stobbe, *Discovering the Mind of a Woman* (Nashville, Tenn.: Oliver Nelson, 1995), 143–44.

20 Robertson McQuilkin, *A Promise Kept* (Wheaton, Ill.: Tyndale House Publishers, 1998), 32–33.

21 H. Norman Wright, *How to Really Love Your Wife* (Ann Arbor, Mich.: Vine Books, 1995), 96.

Marriage Alive International, Inc., founded by husband-wife team Claudia and David Arp, MSW, is a nonprofit marriage- and family-enrichment ministry dedicated to providing resources, seminars, and training to empower churches to help build better marriages and families. The Arps are marriage and family educators, popular speakers, award-winning authors, and frequent contributors to print and broadcast media. They have appeared as marriage experts on programs such as *Today, CBS This Morning,* and *Focus on the Family.* Their Marriage Alive seminar is in great demand across the U.S. and in Europe.

The Mission of Marriage Alive is to identify, train, and empower leaders who invest in others by building strong marriage and family relationships through the integration of biblical truth, contemporary research, practical application, and fun.

Our Resources and Services
- Marriage and family books and small-group resources
- Video-based educational programs including *10 Great Dates to Energize Your Marriage* and *Second Half of Marriage*
- Marriage, pre-marriage, and parenting seminars, including *Before You Say "I Do," Marriage Alive, Second Half of Marriage,* and *Empty Nesting*
- Coaching, mentoring, consulting, training, and leadership development

CONTACT MARRIAGE ALIVE INTERNATIONAL AT WWW.MARRIAGEALIVE.COM OR (888) 690-6667.

The Smalley Relationship Center, founded by Dr. Gary Smalley, offers many varied resources to help people strengthen their marriage and family relationships. The Center provides marriage enrichment products, conferences, training material, articles, and clinical services—all designed to make your most important relationships *successful* relationships.

The Mission of the Smalley Relationship Center is to increase marriage satisfaction and lower the divorce rate by providing a deeper level of care. We want to help couples build strong, successful, and satisfying marriages.

Resources and Services:
- Nationwide conferences: Love Is a Decision, Marriage for a Lifetime
- Counseling services: Couples Intensive program, phone counseling
- Video series, including *Keys to Loving Relationships, Homes of Honor,* and *Secrets to Lasting Love*
- Small group leadership guide
- Articles on marriage, parenting, and stepfamilies
- Smalley Counseling Center provides counseling, national intensives, and more for couples in crisis

CONTACT SMALLEY RELATIONSHIP CENTER AT WWW.SMALLEYONLINE.COM OR 1-800-84-TODAY.